THERE'S A TREE OF LIFE INSIDE OF ME

Written by
Lindi Masters

Illustrated by
Lizzie Masters

Published by

Written by
Lindi Masters©

Illustrated by
Lizzie Masters©

"THERE'S A TREE OF LIFE INSIDE OF ME"
Copyright© 2020

Story written by Lindi Masters
Illustrated and Designed by Lizzie Masters

Special thanks to our mentors and friends Ian Clayton and Grant Mahoney, without whom we wouldn't have explored these Realms.
This edition published by SERAPH CREATIVE in 2021.
ISBN 978-1-922428-18-9

All rights reserved© No part of this publication may be reproduced, stored in a retrieval system or transmitted, in any form or by any means, electronic, mechanical, photocopying, recording or otherwise, without the prior permission of the copyright holder. No part of this book, artwork included may be used or reproduced in any manner without the written permission of the publisher.

Lindi Masters   Lizzie Masters

THERE IS A TRIBE OF
LIFE INSIDE OF ME

This Book belongs to:

_____

My body has a Tree of Life inside of it. It has many different points in it.
My body is the Temple of the Holy Spirit.

When I pray over the different points in my body, it brings alignment to my body. Alignment means to bring into line and proper position.

Did you know that your head is a gate and has a crown?
When I pray over my head, I bring alignment.

Lift up your heads, oh you gates
Psalm 24:9

I pray over my right ear which is a point in my body.
This point is called Wisdom.
Thank you for Wisdom in my body Yeshua.

Blessed are those who find Wisdom
Proverbs 3:13

My left ear is an alignment point in my body too. This point is called understanding. Thank you Yeshua for giving me understanding.

Call Understanding your intimate friend
Proverbs 7:4(b)

When I pray over the point in my chest, I bring alignment. This point is called Knowledge.
Knowledge is like glue that sticks information together.
Wisdom and Understanding come together in my Knowledge point.

My belly is an alignment point in my body called Glory. My emotions are here and sometimes I feel butterflies or excited or sad in my belly. I pray over my belly to bring alignment and peace.

Whoever believes in me, as the scripture has said, out of their belly shall flow rivers of living waters
John 7:38

On my right hip is a point called Victory. When I pray over this point it brings alignment and order into my body.

But thanks be to God! He gives us the victory through Yeshua
1Cor 15:57

I like to pray over my left point in my body, which is on my left hip. This point releases awe, which is wonderment and amazement, into my body.

Everyone kept feeling a sense of awe and many wonders and signs were taking place through the Apostles
Acts 2:43

Below my belly button is a point that also brings alignment to my body. This point brings creativity from Yahweh into my body.

Creativity is also part of my imagination. Imagination has doors that we can go through and engage in Heaven, with Yeshua.

At my knees and feet is an alignment point.
When I pray over these areas of my body I bring rest into my body. It also grounds me and the earth, into Heaven.

For the earnest expectation of the creation eagerly waits for the revealing of the Sons of God
Romans 8:19

My body has a Tree of Life
inside of it.
I love my body.
I am wonderfully made.
I am kind.
I am strong.
My body is the Temple of the
Holy Spirit.

www.ingramcontent.com/pod-product-compliance
Lightning Source LLC
Chambersburg PA
CBHW050758110526
44588CB00002B/47